IMAGES
of America

MISSIONS OF SAN FRANCISCO BAY

This portrayal of coastal natives was painted in 1816 by Ludwig Andrevitch Choris (1795–1828), a historically important Ukrainian-born expedition artist. The *balsas* crafted of tule reeds featured several innovations, including a pointed prow and double-bladed paddles. The boats could carry up to four people along the shores and from island to island in the bay. The striped blanket shown being worn by the passenger at center was made by female neophytes at the missions. (Library of Congress.)

ON THE COVER: Posed in front of Mission San Francisco Solano in Sonoma, the proud owner of a new 1928 Hudson chose the final northern stop on El Camino Real and the last stop of the chain of 21 missions as a memorable backdrop. (Anderson family collection.)

IMAGES
of America

MISSIONS OF SAN FRANCISCO BAY

Robert A. Bellezza

ARCADIA
PUBLISHING

ISBN 978-0-7385-9684-6

Published by Arcadia Publishing
Charleston, South Carolina

Printed in the United States of America

Library of Congress Control Number: 2013946444

For all general information, please contact Arcadia Publishing:
Telephone 843-853-2070
Fax 843-853-0044
E-mail sales@arcadiapublishing.com
For customer service and orders:
Toll-Free 1-888-313-2665

Visit us on the Internet at www.arcadiapublishing.com

To my son, Tony, and daughter, Tara,
for sharing and making our own California history.

CONTENTS

ACKNOWLEDGMENTS

The Library of Congress Prints & Photographs Online Collection supplied the majority of images within this volume and makes possible a review of California's founding architectural landmarks practically lost through centuries of age, deterioration, and neglect. California's mission buildings were rescued only after the majority had suffered the effects of earthquakes, irreversible weathering, and ruin to their adobe walls. By the beginning of the 20th century, there had been efforts to preserve the earliest missions, often built and decorated entirely by California natives. The work employing the Civilian Conservation Corps (CCC) and photographers from the 1933 New Deal documented the progress or decay of the many iconic structures through the Historic American Buildings Survey.

Unless otherwise indicated, all images are courtesy of the Library of Congress, Historic American Buildings Survey/Historic American Engineering Record/Historic American Landscapes Survey.

Several photographs within this volume are released for the first time from vintage glass plate negatives in my collection and the Anderson family collection. Many up-to-date mission photographs featured in chapter seven are from my visits to each area.

A compliment goes to the Sonoma County Historical Society, in particular Sandi Hansen, and the overwhelming archive of material she oversees at the Depot Museum in Sonoma.

The founder and president of the Alta California missions, Miguel Josep Serra was born in Petra, Majorca, one of the Balearic Islands, located some 150 miles off the coast of the Spanish mainland. His religious name of Junípero was chosen after a contemporary and lesser known devotee of St. Francis Assisi. I am truly pleased that this book's release coincides with the 300th anniversary of his birth, November 24, 1713.

INTRODUCTION

The convergence of settlers by land and sea at San Diego's harbor in 1769 brought European colonization to Alta California. The establishment of a historic settlement and presidio was followed by a 54-year turbulent era of Spanish mission culture leading the way into uncharted northern territories. Captains Fernando de Rivera y Moncada and Gasper de Portolá, accompanied by Franciscan padres with initial expeditions along El Camino Real, or "The Royal Highway," opened nearly 650 miles. The Franciscan clergy supervised expanding industries and a prosperous cultivation of crops and livestock. Generations of native Indian neophytes were assimilated within the massive mission quadrangles. Spanish control was ceded with the transition of power from the victory in 1821 by the Republic of Mexico, ending the long lineage. The 21st mission and last in Alta California, Mission San Francisco Solano, had been dedicated by Fr. José Altimira on July 4, 1823, at El Pueblo de Sonoma.

THE TRAIL OF DISCOVERY

Mexico City's viceroy, José de Galvez, planned the first colonies in Alta California with Spanish missionary Fr. Junípero Serra to establish territorial defenses of Spain's uncharted possession. Over many decades, seafaring navigators charting California's coast were followed by land expeditions. On July 16, 1769, with soldiers, conquistadors, and new settlers, the Spanish Franciscan padres began to explore California's immense upper territories. Mission settlements in Baja California, begun by Padre Juan María Salvatierra in 1697, were replicated with a series of 21 Alta California missions, employing generations of mission Indian neophytes as the builders. A first mission of simple mud-covered brush *enramadas* grew into buildings of elaborate stonework and adobe brick, centrally available in pueblo quadrangles. The impressive buildings of crafted stone, adobe brick, and clay tile were made by skilled Spanish builders aided by apprentice native neophytes. Miguel Josep Serra was born in 1713 on Majorca, a distant Spanish island, in the town of Petra. He took the name Junípero and became a devotee of the Franciscan order, traveling as a missionary in 1749. He first visited Puerto Rico, and then sailed to Vera Cruz, Mexico. After landing, Father Serra displayed an act of tremendous religious zeal, choosing to walk 275 miles through the deep jungles to reach the spiritual seat of the New World and the Franciscan San Fernando College in Mexico City. In 1750, Father Serra began his work within the jungles of Mexico, emerging into Baja, where he was quickly elevated by the church to mission president in 1767. Providing great experience and knowledge of agriculture and an unrelenting strength as a day laborer, Father Serra also displayed his unique talents as a linguist and educator. He mixed his days of farming, building, spinning, weaving, and sewing with theatrical reenactments of biblical events, performed to enlighten native neophytes. At 56 years of age, Father Serra began making plans to travel by sea to meet the Baja governor, explorer Don Gaspar de Portolá, in Monterey. Portolá assembled a group of padres, leatherjacket soldiers, and scouting parties and established Alta California's new northern capital, presidio, and mission on June 3, 1770, with great fanfare. Sgt. José de Ortega, pathfinder of Portolá's expedition, first sighted San Francisco's vast harbor in 1769. Juan Manuel de Ayala commanded a voyage to San Francisco Bay and charted the area in 1775, after several other attempts by Spanish explorers. Lt. Col. Juan Bautista de Anza marched over 1,000 miles to the Pacific, bringing 235 settlers out of the Mexican Sonoran Desert, through the sands of the Mojave Desert, and onto Alta California's stunning harbor and bay, named for the Franciscan order's patron, St. Francis of Assisi.

A MISSION FOR ST. FRANCIS

In 1776, the founding of San Francisco occurred serendipitously less than a week from America's Independence Day of July 4. De Anza located the new presidio site near a small lake and stream christened Arroyo de los Dolores, honoring Our Lady of Sorrows, and venerated the mission with the designation of the Virgin Mary on the last Friday of Lent. De Anza brought with him settlers from Sinaloa and Sonora, Mexico, including carpenters, masons, farmers, and families with farm animals and supplies. Following the dedication of Mission San Francisco de Asís, under an order from Mexico City's viceroy to secure more Spanish settlements within the territories of Alta California, Mission Santa Clara became the eighth in California on January 12, 1777, established by Fr. Junípero Serra at the edge of Rio Guadalupe near the meadows. Nearby, El Pueblo de San José de Guadalupe became the first town chartered in California, founded by José Joaquín Moraga on November 29, 1777. Expanding to the west in 1791, Mission Santa Cruz was established and located on a hilltop overlooking the town and sea. Today, rare original housing known as the Neary-Rodriguez or School Street Adobe, once quarters for neophytes adjacent to the original mission's grounds, is still standing. The Mission del Gloriosísima Patriarca San José was founded June 11, 1797, by Fr. Fermín Francisco de Lasuén and was a success, converting a total of 6,736 neophytes to the church by the 1830s. At first, Mission San Rafael, Arcángel, was built as a hospital and *asistencia*, established by Fr. Vincente de Sarría on December 14, 1817. The warm, dry environment, with its curative effects, became a refuge to the victims of diseases now rampant at Mission Dolores. The final Spanish settlement of Mission San Francisco de Solano was founded on July 4, 1823, by Fr. José Altimira, and the new mission chapel was built in 1840 by Gen. Mariano Guadalupe Vallejo, integrated within El Pueblo de Sonoma. Sonoma Valley was the final scene of the Spanish mission era and became the last stop on El Camino Real.

Passing of the Mission Era

In 1811, the decentralization of Spanish power spawned unrest among its colonists, who rose up in the Mexican War of Independence, and led to the sudden loss of support for the mission hierarchy in Alta California. The colonies' self-supporting neophyte numbers were steadily declining from decades of skirmishes with soldiers, desertions, and diseases. Mexican *vaqueros*, known as Californios, were encouraged to migrate through Baja's southern settlements into Alta California for livestock grazing. Conflicts between Spanish soldiers and neophyte families ignited fierce rebellions and led to deterioration of mission conditions. Local Ohlone, Yokut, and other coastal tribes of San Francisco Bay experienced the loss of industries, commerce, and culture. A new governor, Manuel Micheltorena, was sent to Monterey to begin granting titles of rancho properties, often rewarding governmental service or paying back loans. Even enlisting Americans like Swiss immigrant Capt. John Augustus Sutter, the new governor began retiring the old guard of the Mexican military. Its most prominent citizen was Gen. Mariano Guadalupe Vallejo, the military commandant of the north, who continued organizing mission populations and carved out an elaborate empire, erecting El Casa Grande, the new military headquarters in the pueblo of Sonoma. Vallejo ordered a new adobe chapel at Mission San Francisco Solano in 1840. His empire included his enormous two-storied adobe and personal *rancho* in Petaluma, which hired local Indians. Opposition was organized against him by Juan Bautista Alvarado, California governor in 1836, who hastened 400 citizens in an attack to capture the Monterey garrison, seizing control from the corrupt military. Governor Micheltorena would eventually cede power in 1845 to the last Mexican governor, Pio Pico, and José Castro, military commandant. During the final years of Mexican rule, Pio Pico divided and sold mission properties, paying off debts or granting favors to family members. One exception to all early missions of California, Mission Santa Bárbara, survived under continuous Franciscan residency, as many old Spanish adobes had deteriorated and been ravaged by earthquakes and fires. By June 14, 1846, US Army captain John C. Frémont backed the Bear Flag Revolt at Sonoma Plaza as 33 American volunteers captured the commandant, General Vallejo. On July 7, 1846, the commander of the Pacific Squadron, Commodore John Drake Sloat, raised the American flag, finalizing the Battle of Monterey. Days later, Capt. Thomas Fallon led a small force of 22 volunteers from Santa Cruz to capture El Pueblo de San José on July 11. Fallon received the American flag from Sloat, raising it over the pueblo on July 14, declaring the California Republic's allegiance to the United States. Frémont captured Santa Bárbara, trudging over the wet mountain passes of Santa Ynez, in December 1846. The Treaty of Guadalupe Hidalgo was signed on February 2, 1848, ceding control of California to the United States, and California was admitted as a state in 1850.

One

Our Beloved Dolores

Mission San Francisco de Asís

Fr. Junípero Serra's request in 1767 for a mission to honor St. Francis had been answered after Don Gaspar de Portolá's search passed Monterey Bay in 1769. His scouts discovered what seemed a vast "arm of the sea," and a port for St. Francis was revealed. Lt. Col. Juan Bautista de Anza led a founding party on June 27, 1776, to a rise near a small lake and stream he named Dolores to honor Madre Dolorosa, "The Sorrowful Mother." Fr. Francisco Palóu celebrated founding mass. Mission San Francisco de Asís church moved in 1783 to its current site and was completed in 1791. It stands 1,100 feet east of the mission's original location. (Anderson family collection.)

In 1579, Sir Francis Drake's landing at California's northern shoreline revealed an expansive landscape surrounded by native residents at Point Reyes. Spain's recognition of safe harbors in the northern territories was needed for sea traders, including the British, Russian, and other foreign flags. In 1595, Sebastian Rodriguez Cermeno, Portuguese captain and commander of the Spanish ship *San Augustin*, had orders to explore the coast and attempted a landing at Drake's Estero, Point Reyes, during a massive storm. His ship was pummeled, its cargo from China and the Philippines breaking loose and spilling into pieces that were recovered by the native Coastal Miwok. Cermeno bravely attempted to save his men, employing makeshift boats to wend his way through inland bays and marching overland to reach Acapulco, Mexico, in one year. One seafaring merchant, Sebastián Vizcaíano, had sailed past the great bay left undiscovered in 1603, hidden by constant fog. In 1775, Don Fernando marked the mission's site named for the patron of the Franciscan order. Spanish explorer Juan Manuel de Ayala followed with the first voyage through San Francisco's narrow Golden Gate on August 5, 1775. He then spent six weeks exploring the bay's features, its appearance then not unlike this lantern slide view from around 1912. (Author's collection.)

Explorer Gaspar de Portolá named a small stream Arroyo de Nuestra Señora de los Dolores, honoring Our Lady of Sorrows. The Mission San Francisco de Asís's first mass was celebrated on June 29, 1776, by Fr. Francisco Palóu, coworker and biographer of Fr. Junípero Serra. After official documents arrived, the mission was consecrated on October 9, 1776, and became the sixth of Alta California's Spanish missions.

The Franciscan control of Alta California's missions continued during the Mexican War for Independence beginning in 1811. New challenges to Mission San Francisco de Asís came with the arrival of Fr. José Altimira and his plan to move many neophytes away to the Sonoma Valley and establish Mission San Francisco Solano, leaving Mission Dolores without clergy. In answer, Father President José Señán retained Mission Dolores in 1822, giving Mission San Rafael, Arcángel, full mission status and agreeing to a new California mission, Mission San Francisco Solano, which was founded by Father Altimira on July 4, 1823.

This 1865 photograph shows Mission Dolores, San Francisco's oldest building, just 15 years after California's entry to the Union as the 31st state. The adjacent mission *convento* quarters extending south were removed by 1875 and replaced by a Gothic Revival church, then the present basilica.

Mission Dolores was consecrated the day after Father Palóu laid the first brick for the new church, April 25, 1782. He was accompanied by his assistant, Father Santa María, and the administrator of Mission Santa Clara, Fr. José Antonio Murguía. The historic Mission Dolores church is the first and oldest survivor of San Francisco's classic architecture.

Pictured in 1898, and commonly known as Mission Dolores after its dedication in 1776, the Mission San Francisco de Asís was originally a log and thatch roof building located a block and a half away. The present-day church remains intact, with its principal altar brought by ship from Mexico in 1796. It was a survivor of the devastating earthquake and fire of 1906.

This 1860s photograph reveals that San Francisco was growing as America's most popular western destination. To the right, the old Mansion House had many uses over the years, housing a brewery, two taverns, a dancing room, a saloon, private lodgings, and a hospital, while maintaining the church as a place of worship. Eventually, the old house was leveled to construct a Gothic brick church; the current basilica replaced it in 1918.

This portrait from 1870 reveals the Mission Dolores grounds confined within a city block as the town began to grow rapidly around it. An adobe wall was built later to enclose the redefined cemetery. Graves were moved within remaining church grounds or carried to other locations.

Presented to the mission by Viceroy of Mexico Antonio de Mendoza, the central bell was cast in 1792 and is the subject of this 1936 photograph. Over centuries, mission bells were strapped by leather thongs to a counterweight at the top of a wooden crossbar to easily swing in place.

The austere nave of Mission Dolores is pictured in this vintage postcard. Although the first stone was laid on April 26, 1782, the present church was completed after Father Serra's lifetime. Several cherished artifacts once used by him remain in the mission's museum.

Mission Dolores's eastward-facing entry is a feature of many early church structures, aligned to illuminate the building and altars during sunrise. Although many improvements upgraded the structure over the years, it remains identical in appearance to its earliest days.

The Mission Dolores cemetery (above, foreground) was the final resting place of many pioneer settlers of California, including Lt. José Joaquin Moraga, leader of the expedition that founded San Francisco. Below, the Victorian church of 1876 fills the perimeter of what was once the old adobe Mansion House. Although Mission Dolores remained intact, the adjoining brick church was declared unsafe after the 1906 earthquake.

The evolution of the city is revealed in the photograph above, taken prior to the completion of the Victorian brick church of 1876. Although confined to a significantly smaller tract of property, the city's oldest survivor, the Mission Dolores church and its interior, remained unchanged. Soon, the corner of Dolores and Sixteenth Streets defined the mission property boundaries.

The entire 1876 Victorian brick church had been rendered unsafe by the San Francisco earthquake of 1906, and was razed in 1913. The present grand Mission Dolores Basilica replaced it in 1918, slowed by delays due to World War I.

This photograph from 1898 offers a dramatic view of the modern parish church of 1876 overshadowing the aged Mission Dolores. Beneath the floor of the old mission church lies the grave of José Joaquín Moraga, the founder of San Jose's pueblo and leader of the first group of settlers to San Francisco, accompanied in 1776 by the mission's founder, Fr. Francisco Palóu. (Southwest Museum of the American Indian Collection.)

Popularly named Mission Dolores after the nearby creek and lake, which in time was filled and paved over, the church was dedicated in 1776 by Fr. Francisco Palóu. The mission's original site was about 1,100 feet away. The church's design is unique among all California missions. It measured 114 feet long by 22 feet wide with four-foot-thick adobe walls. Nearly 36,000 sun-dried adobe bricks were used to complete the mission's walls. Redwood beams support the shaved poles of the roof, lashed together with rawhide, and they remain in place today. This photograph from 1936 shows the church facade as it appeared more than 100 years ago.

The mission property was transferred to an Indian pueblo in 1834 and was among the first of the secularized missions. By March 3, 1851, Pres. James Buchanan restored four acres of original holdings of Mission Dolores to Bishop Joseph Alemany. Wooden planked roadways to the Mission District led to bull and bear fights, gambling, drinking, and other entertainment, although the mission church continued as a place of prayer.

Within this small baptismal niche, the font stands on the tiles from the floor at Mission San Francisco de Asís. A larger font replicating one at Father Serra's birthplace in Spain replaced the pedestal font in 1995.

Architectural influences from the 1915 Panama-California Exposition, held at San Diego's Balboa Park, were added to the Mission Dolores Basilica's spires and facade during a remodel in 1926. Seen here in a vintage postcard view, the ornate structure appears as it looks today. The basilica adjoins the original grounds of the early mission. (Author's collection.)

The cemetery at Mission Dolores extended beyond the edges of the city block in the days of the earliest settlement. As the developing city grew around it, many graves had to be moved within the current grounds of the mission or to other city cemeteries.

The south bell swings within the church's front wall *espandaña*, hung traditionally with rawhide thongs. The original bells' names, south to north, are San Martin, San Francisco, and San Jose. They were cast from 1792 to 1797 and were memorialized by California poet Bret Harte in 1868 in a nostalgic tribute to the mission's romantic history.

Access to the Mission Dolores attic is limited. The structural integrity of the mission has remained intact for more than 200 years. The supporting redwood truss beams are bound with rawhide thongs, as in the original roof.

This vintage view shows Mission Dolores in 1936. Father Cambrón designed the church in the southeast corner of the quadrangle, and by 1782 the mud for the adobe was taken from the banks of Dolores Creek near today's Dolores and Dorland Streets. The foundations are four feet wide and four feet deep and thought to be of stone quarried from Mint Hill.

On the south side of the Mission Dolores church, the mission cemetery was the final resting place of many California founders, including 5,000 Ohlone and Miwok natives. Many graves were consolidated after smaller boundaries for the mission were imposed by the developing city. (Author's collection.)

This historic marker at the mission marks the grave of Gov. Don Luis Antonio Argüello, the first native-born governor of Alta California from 1822 to 1825. During Mexico's war with Spain, Governor Argüello presided over a decreasing neophyte population, as 1,200 dwindled down to 219. Many neophytes were relocated at other missions, such as the asistencia San Rafael, Arcángel, near Mission Dolores, established as a health retreat and becoming a full mission by 1822.

Gov. Don Luis Antonio Argüello's grave marker toppled over in the 1906 earthquake but was righted and repaired. His father, José Darío Argüello, and mother, Maria Ygnacia Moraga, were members of distinguished and influential families of Alta California settlers.

Portrayed in a vintage postcard, the oldest building within the city of San Francisco was severely affected by secularization after 1834. Its properties were sold in 1845, and Fr. Antonio Dantí's hold weakened to 280 mission Indian neophytes. Decreasing numbers left just its women and children. The padres' records revealed 62,000 deaths and 29,000 births of native neophytes between 1779 and 1833.

The original church at Mission Dolores withstood the severe 1906 San Francisco earthquake and fire, while the adjoining 1870s church was damaged beyond repair. Construction on a replacement for the brick church was started in 1913, delayed by World War I until 1918. Mission Dolores was granted minor basilica status in 1952.

The domed ceiling is rarely photographed and documents early neophytes' decorative frescos and how they were made from vegetable dyes and minerals.

The cemetery today features an Ohlone Indian ethno-botanical garden with examples of native plants and culturally significant flowers, shrubs, and herbs. Artifacts include a tule hut and a memorial to their villages. By 1820, Mission Dolores converts had declined, leaving mostly women, elders, and children. (Author's collection.)

The statue of St. Francis was honored in a solitary space and niche within the nave. St. Francis, the founder of the Franciscan order, lived between 1181 and 1226 in Assisi, Italy, abandoning a life of luxury for poverty. He was canonized as a saint on July 16, 1228. He had been known to receive visions, later revealing stigmata emulating the bleeding wounds of Christ.

Altars at each side feature revered statuary, among the finest examples of elaborate Spanish-Mexican carvings brought to the mission in 1810. Dyes decorating the mission were reproduced using the native color schemes and accurate examples of the early mission culture. The church was added as the sixth mission in Alta California, and the present Mission San Francisco de Asís was completed in 1791.

Fr. Junípero Serra, founder of California's mission chain and Mission San Francisco de Asís, gazes over the descendants of devotees following him. This sculpture by Arthur Putnam was installed in 1918 in the center of the cemetery gardens.

After 1834, the city of San Francisco entered a secularized era. Daily life at the mission included bullfights and frontier justice carried out in the streets. Depictions of the era were included with a series of drawings of all the missions made after 1877 by Oriana Weatherbee Day (1838–1886), an American artist.

This vintage postcard features one of San Francisco's oldest attractions. Over decades, a world audience has enjoyed the historical significance of Mission Dolores. (Author's collection.)

The interior of Mission Dolores features intricately carved statuary, shown here in 1936. The side altar features scenes from the lives of great saints, including, from left to right, San Juan Capistrano, San Antonio de Padua, and San Buenaventura.

Father Serra's glossy image was used during World War II. This news photograph shows the April 26, 1944, launching of the SS *Mission Dolores*, a tanker built by Marinship Corporation in a Sausalito shipyard and named for the bay's famed mission. The superimposed statue of Fr. Junípero Serra lends the image a dramatic effect.

The chapel altar within the Mission Dolores nave has remained unchanged throughout centuries. The ornate baroque-style reredos was added after 1796 and was discovered blocking from view for 200 years an authentic painted mural measuring 22 by 20 feet of religious imagery, reportedly the best preserved example of indigenous art from the period of first contact with Europeans. The mural was digitally imaged after the year 2000.

This postcard view shows the church nave of the adjacent Mission Dolores Basilica. It replaced the Victorian brick church after structural failure during the earthquake of 1906. The present basilica was completed by 1918 and again remodeled in 1926.

Ludwig Andrevitch Choris (1795–1828), while traveling through San Francisco in October 1816, depicted the Mission Dolores plaza, a center of activity filled with festivities, music, and dancing fully accepted by the friars. Choris painted colorful gambling games and mission life as he observed the important components of the coastal natives' lives. Among traditional dances were the coyote dance, the dove dance, and the bear dance. Dancers painted themselves with vegetable dyes, hematite, cinnabar, and white clay, and wore necklaces of shell beads. Choris studied the Ohlone, meaning "the abalone people," which is closer to their own conception of ancestral identity than Costeño, a Spanish term.

Louis Andrevitch Choris, a historically important Ukrainian-born expedition artist and traveler, portrayed many of the earliest known scenes of California's natives during his journey to San Francisco in 1816 as a pictorial journalist.

A memorial Ohlone home exists at the Mission Dolores cemetery in tribute to the native culture's mission era, when neophytes lived simple lifestyles in bound huts of wetlands tule reeds. After 1819, over 40,000 coastal natives were decimated by disease. Gen. Mariano Vallejo and his brother, Salvador, carved a personal empire and created backlash from settlers and aboriginal communities as far north as Healdsburg, as many native tribes valiantly resisted but were eventually overcome by the steady migrations from the California Gold Rush in 1849.

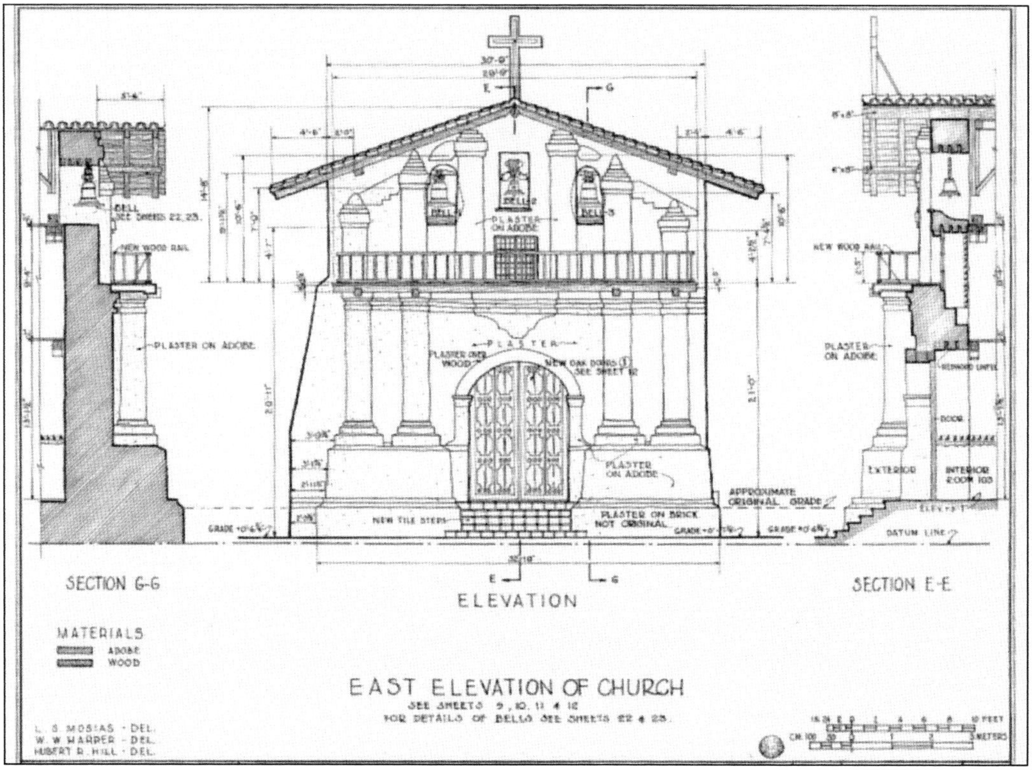

In 1768, José de Gálvez, the inspector general of Mexico City, informed Fr. Junípero Serra of selected names for the missions he would establish in Alta California. Serra expressed disappointment that Saint Francis had been neglected, asking: "And, for our founder St. Francis there is no Mission?" To which Gálvez replied: "If St. Francis desires a mission, let him show us his harbor and he shall have one." The legendary promise of a mission for Saint Francis eventually was realized in June 1776 with Mission San Francisco de Asís.

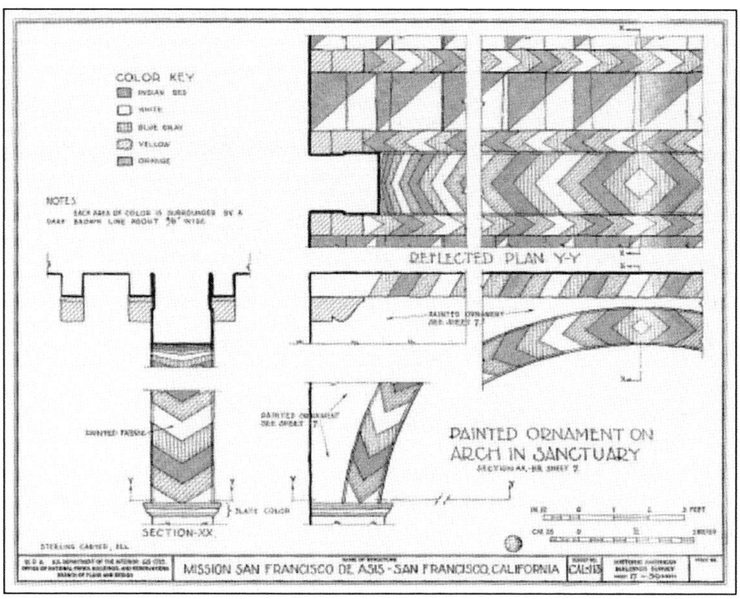

Two

MEADOWLANDS MISSION
MISSION SANTA CLARA DE ASÍS

Founded on January 12, 1777, by Fr. Junípero Serra, Mission Santa Clara de Asís was the eighth of Alta California's growing mission lineage. The first church was built on the banks of Rio Guadalupe on a spot sighted by explorer Lt. Col. Juan Bautista de Anza. After flooding twice, it was moved to the present site. The current mission building, a replica of the church from 1825 as painted by Augustin Dávila, was destroyed by fire in 1926, then rebuilt in 1929. (Anderson family collection.)

Santa Clara College became the first place of higher learning in California, run by Jesuit missionaries and chartered in April 1855. The old mission church site of 1825 is surrounded by the campus, and pictured is the fifth mission church. It was dramatically consumed in 1926 by an electrical fire that started in the south belfry. The present Mission Santa Clara de Asís was rebuilt by 1929 and resembles the original design, decorated by Augustin Dávila. The third church consecrated by Fr.

The Mission Santa Clara nave and exterior were first painted decoratively by the skilled Mexican artisan Augustin Dávila. After rebuilding and painting, replicating his ceiling design effectively simulates the original from 1825. Within the niches of the present day church, the patron, Saint Clare, a contemporary of Saint Francis, stands in the center as leader of the Franciscan order, the Poor Clares. (Southwest Museum of the American Indian Collection.)

Junípero Serra in 1784, it was finished just months before his death. The cornerstone contained artifacts from the church given by Father Serra and later recovered accidently in 1911 during gas pipe excavations. The college was designated a university in 1912, when schools of engineering and law were added. (Santa Clara University Archives and Special Collections.)

This lantern slide from around 1912 depicts Mission Santa Clara de Asís with a vintage auto of the day. The mission was named in honor of Saint Clare (1194–1263) of Assisi, Italy, a follower and contemporary of Saint Francis. In 1851, the mission church was ceded by the Franciscans and became a Jesuit mission and the nucleus of a new college. The Maryknoll Fathers took charge of the mission in 1929. (Author's collection.)

Mission Santa Clara de Asís is pictured in 1911 in the center of the University of Santa Clara, California's first established college. The church was moved three times after its founding due to floods and earthquakes; the final site was chosen in 1818.

Delicate decorated ceiling paintings are the work of Augustin Dávila, an established painter from Mexico. The loss of the wooden ceiling and building after the 1926 conflagration left only photographs to aid the reconstruction of the church. (Santa Clara University Archives and Special Collections.)

This photograph shows Mission Santa Clara de Asís's church, constructed in 1825 and remodeled in 1885, when a matched second campanile was built and the entire church veneered with an ornate Italianate facade. It was the fifth building following its founding in 1777 by Father Serra. By 1839, the first campanile tower of adobe had been replaced by a wooden one and rebuilt again in 1862. (Santa Clara University Archives and Special Collections.)

Only a few relics survived after fires in 1909 and 1913 and the final decimation, the fire of 1926. Recovered relics include Indian-carved sanctuary chairs and statuary. (Santa Clara University Archives and Special Collections.)

A devastating fire consuming the church occurred on October 24, 1926, completely engulfing and leveling the building. It left only one adobe room and a partial wall from the original mission period. The fire's origins pointed to an accidental electrical short ignited inside the belfry.

The church of Mission Santa Clara de Asís was restored after the accidental 1926 fire. A redwood cross made with timber brought from the Santa Cruz mountains was hewn to replace the original from 1777, and a repository for old relics of the first mission cross was created. The 1907 celebration planted a new one six feet deep and standing 24 feet high. The 1926 fire started within the north belfry of the church, causing the bells to fall and alerting surrounding residents of the danger.

The fifth church was begun in 1822, dedicated in 1825, and remodeled in 1861 and 1887 (above). Fray Tomas de la Peña, accompanied by the lieutenant commander of the San Francisco Presidio, began his journey in 1777 to establish Mission Santa Clara de Asís. Fr. José Murguía arrived days later with liturgical items and supplies for the first mission, built of logs and dedicated on January 12, 1777. The church was destroyed two years later by flooding, and a new temporary church was constructed on higher ground. It was blessed by Fr. Junípero Serra on November 11, 1779. On November 19, 1781, at the church's present site, an elaborate ritual laying the cornerstone of the larger adobe church was performed by Father Serra. He celebrated mass assisted by Fathers Peña and Palóu in a dedication ceremony on May 15, 1784. Enclosed in a cavity of the cornerstone were a Spanish crucifix, religious images, and coins to signify the church treasury. The adobe church was damaged by an earthquake, and a fourth church was begun in 1818. The building became an Indian boys' residence, then a dance hall after secularization in the 1830s. (Santa Clara University Archives and Special Collections.)

The river flooded the settlement of 1779, and it was abandoned soon after. This photograph from 1900 depicts a commemorative occasion marked by parishioners' homage to the founding spot, where Fray de la Peña celebrated the first mass near the Guadalupe River on January 12, 1777.

Lt. Col. Juan Bautista de Anza gave the name Rio de Nuestra Señora de Guadalupe to the river flowing at a fertile site soon after his discovery of the trail to San Francisco's peninsula in 1776. The site at the river had been chosen for the first two churches built of logs and a temporary adobe quadrangle of a granary, dwellings, and a guardhouse.

The old adobe church of 1825 is framed in this 1849 photograph that documents designs carried over to the modern church facade, known to be painted in brilliant hues by Augustin Dávila in 1835. Below, the campanile, weakened by heavy rains in 1839, was replaced with battened wooden siding. The adobe church walls were replaced in 1884 and framed in wood to preserve the old building as well as widen the church.

Mission Santa Clara is set today within a peaceful garden of mission vines and several varieties of palm trees. At the first settlement, several Indians were caught stealing and feasting on mules from the mission ranch. The culprits took refuge in the tules and then fired volleys of arrows at soldiers, who retaliated. The killing of three led to the capture of the rest.

This view of Mission Santa Clara de Asís's altar shows its *reredos* panels of sacred statues at the rear. Saint Clare, the patron of Mission Santa Clara de Asís, is posed within the central niche bearing a monstrance, the sacred multi-spired vessel containing the sacrament host used in displaying her legendary courage defending her native village from intruders.

A dedication mass at the new church fills the newly completed replica in 1929. Seen below is the Mission Santa Clara de Asís church nave of 1825 as it appeared prior to the devastating fire of 1926. (Above, Santa Clara University Archives and Special Collections; below, Southwest Museum of the American Indian Collection.)

The altar and carved oratory pulpit are pictured prior to the fire that destroyed the church of 1825. The church had been previously remodeled in 1861 and 1887. Several statues were saved from devastation during the fire of 1926, including the large crucifix of the side altar.

Native clam diggers of a Northern Californian tribe continued their traditions through the centuries. Mission neophytes were dramatically impacted by European influences, and gradually, the cultural habits of the assimilated Native Americans faded as their reliance on agricultural crops grown by the mission fathers increased.

Edward S. Curtis (1868–1952), a renowned photographer, sought out the disappearing Indians in their native habitats. Mission fathers were presented with a large population of over 1,500 Ohlone, Yokut, and Sierra Miwok ready to join the church in 1795. Nearly an entire village of 400 appeared in one year for baptism rites. The fathers journeyed inland, discovering Miwok natives with different customs and languages who also embraced mission life.

The catastrophic fire of 1926 left small salvageable walls of the building and few original artifacts, but students managed to rescue statues, paintings, and other liturgical objects, as well as one of the old mission bells. Careful copies were made of the destroyed Mexican reredos and Dávila's painted ceiling. The replica of the burned church imparts the flavor of the original building it replaced. (Santa Clara University Archives and Special Collections.)

Don Fernando Rivera y Moncada relayed instructions via Father Palóu for Lieutenant Moraga and Fr. Tomas de la Peña to venture south along the bay to establish Mission Santa Clara, the eighth in the Alta California chain. Until the 1870s, it was the parish church of California's first chartered city, the pueblo of San Jose. (Author's collection.)

Less than six months after the mission's founding, Moraga received instructions to begin a civilian pueblo, as migrating citizens waited at the Mission San Gabriel, Arcángel, after de Anza's desert march. El Pueblo de San José was founded near Mission Santa Clara. Rebuilding Mission Santa Clara de Asís after flooding in 1784, the skilled Spanish builders at the new mission grounds created an elaborate quadrangle that served until the earthquake of 1818.

The remains of adobe structures within the walls of the mission were incorporated into the College of Santa Clara as administration buildings and quarters after 1851. The Jesuit friars founded the college in 1851 and were given a charter in 1855.

Santa Clara University, the oldest college in California, was founded in 1851. Today's mission church courtyard is surrounded by remaining structures, including the Adobe Lodge and the old Adobe Wall from 1822, built under the supervision of Fray José Viader and Fray Magín Catalá.

Santa Clara Valley was known as the Llano de los Robles, or Plain of the Oaks, at the time of the mission's founding and was an excellent place for northern defenses from coastal incursions. Full renovations and restoration included an archeological excavation of the site in 1981.

A part of the quadrangle, the Adobe Lodge is open today for catering events and displays paintings from the 1880s by Jesuit Brother Tortore, who served as an art instructor at the University of Santa Clara from 1874 to 1904.

In 1849, Andrew P. Hill depicted the busy life of Mission Santa Clara and its diverse citizenry, sketching the cross from 1777 and the founding church. In the first six months, only three adult natives were baptized into the church. The first church, dwellings, barn, shops, and corrals were developed soon after.

Padre José Viader contributed 40 years to missionary service in Alta California. He was present when the church cornerstone of Mission Santa Clara de Asís was laid. In 1833 he left the country, and Padre Francisco García Diego, the prefect of the Zacatecan Franciscan friars, became his successor. Father Diego afterwards became the first bishop of all California, stationed at Mission Santa Bárbara. The painted ceiling of this period was among many lost decorative paintings during the catastrophic blaze of 1926.

The sixth church of Mission Santa Clara de Asís was dedicated on May 13, 1928, reconstructed with steel beams replicating the original building of 1825—the adobe church with a single bell tower before it had been altered.

The Cathedral Basilica of St. Joseph, a Roman Catholic church in downtown San Jose, was originally built in 1803. The original adobe structure was damaged by earthquakes in 1818 and 1822, and a new adobe church was built from 1835 to 1846. The second church was severely damaged by the 1868 Hayward Fault earthquake, and the third church was built in 1869. The third church was destroyed by fire in 1875 and was replaced by a temporary fourth church, built a few blocks away. The portico entry was completed in 1884, and a large dome was finished in 1885. (Santa Clara University Archives and Special Collections.)

Mission Santa Clara was founded near El Pueblo de San José de Guadalupe, the first civil settlement in Alta California. A small adobe village church was constructed in 1803 and dedicated to Saint Joseph, establishing the first non-mission parish in California. This postcard view of the interior nave at the Cathedral of St. Joseph reveals the ornate dome completed after 1885. Bishop Joseph Sadoc Alemany had dedicated the cathedral's fifth parish church on April 22, 1877. The Vatican bestowed basilica status on the cathedral in 1997. (Author's collection.)

The sixth church of Mission Santa Clara de Asís was dedicated on May 13, 1928. The mission is shown below after 1877 in a drawing by Oriana Weatherbee Day (1838–1886), an American artist. She personified a tradition of artists traveling to view their subject and rendered a series of colorful post-mission portraits documenting California's disappearing heritage. (Above, author's collection.)

Three

Seaside Sanctuary
La Exaltación de la Santa Cruz

Honoring the feast of the Exultation of the Holy Cross, Mission Santa Cruz is Alta California's 12th and is set high on a hilltop overlooking the Pacific. It was founded by Fr. Fermín Francisco de Lasuén on August 28, 1791. Although remote from the coastal native population, 500 friendly neophytes helped build the church and mission properties. After 1821, the neophytes sharply declined in numbers, and buildings fell into ruin. The bell tower collapsed from an earthquake in 1840, and an 1857 earthquake toppled the front wall of the church. An adobe building for housing neophytes remains from 1824 at the far end of the original mission quadrangle. (Author's collection.)

The chapel at Mission Santa Cruz was recreated from a few watercolor paintings of the early historical ruins, and then left to the imagination of architects to replicate. One missionary from 1812, Fr. Andrés Quintana, was discovered dead here in his bed, and was immediately considered a victim of murder. His disciplinary technique had turned fearsome to neophytes, and he is considered the second martyred padre serving the Alta California missions. Governor Figueroa brought the first Mexican missionaries in 1833 to Santa Cruz, and Fr. Antonio Reál succeeded Franciscan Fr. José Jimeno. The mission was the first to be secularized during this period.

A replica of Mission Santa Cruz was designed in 1931 and was greatly influenced by the research of the French artist Leon Trousset and his painting of 1876. The mission neophytes shared cattle stock and received civil liberties as residents of the pueblo they named Figueroa. The name had changed by 1845 to Santa Cruz.

The neophyte population reached 523 at its peak in 1796, one of the lowest of all converted to a California mission. The first to be affected by secularized law, the church fell into ruin, the tower collapsed in 1840, and the front wall collapsed after 1857. The original baptismal font resides within a niche at the right rear of the mission church. Other artifacts were brought from Mission San Carlos de Borreomeo, the closest Spanish mission, including the vestments now given to the museum. As recently as 1936, an original mission statue of Saint Peter cared for by the Rodríguez family was handed back to the church.

Among the founders of Mission Santa Cruz, Fathers Baldomero López and Alonzo Salazar prepared the title pages of the mission registers, now preserved at the mission museum. The first adobe church measured about 30 feet by 112 feet and stood 25 feet high on foundation walls three feet high built of stone.

The Church of the Holy Cross, photographed around 1889, replaced the second church built of wood on the original quadrangle site. After the cornerstone of the first adobe Mission Santa Cruz church was laid on February 27, 1793, it was formally dedicated on May 10, 1794, by Fr. Tomas de la Peña of Santa Clara, aided by five other priests.

This 1932 photograph was taken shortly after completion of the scale replica mission church. To the left, the museum was designed in place of the monastery wing and borders a small interior courtyard and a Spanish fountain. (Southwest Museum of the American Indian Collection.)

A Spanish town across the San Lorenzo River, Villa de Branciforte, was built on pasturing grounds of the Indians. A threat to the mission's crop agriculture, the grazing herds led to tensions among natives, padres, and soldiers, and many neophytes deserted. In 1818, with the threat of French-Argentine privateer Hyppolyte de Bourchard in Monterey Bay, Spanish soldiers dispersed all the valuable mission possessions to other locations or buried them. The communities of the mission completely disappeared in 1841–1842, and everything was regarded as part of Villa de Branciforte.

To replace the ruins of the earliest mission's adobe chapel of 1793, the cornerstone for a new wooden church was laid in 1857 and was used as the parish church until 1898. The present Gothic church replaced it and was built between 1884 and 1889. In 1862, the Daughters of Charity of St. Vincent de Paul opened Holy Cross School, the first educational institution in the parish.

A beautiful replica church was completed in 1931 at the Mission Plaza adjacent to the original adobe site. The citizens of Santa Cruz erected a granite archway in front of the new Church of the Holy Cross to commemorate the founding of Mission Santa Cruz on September 25, 1891. The construction at the original mission site of a brick Gothic church under Rev. Hugh McNamee marked the transition from Mission Santa Cruz to Holy Cross Parish..

Photographed in 1936, an adobe original to the mission period, the Neary-Rodiguez Building at the end of School Street had housed neophytes at Mission Santa Cruz. Later, it was covered with siding and had a second story and other additions added. Today, the restored neophyte housing is open for visitors at Santa Cruz Mission State Historic Park. Ohlone communities identified in present-day Santa Cruz County number several distinct groups, including the Cotoni on the north coast, the Achiasta in the upper San Lorenzo River basin, the Uypi in the area around Santa Cruz, the Sayanta in the Zayante Creek watershed, the Chalocata on the slopes of Loma Prieta and the watershed of upper Soquel Creek, the Aptos in the area now given their name, the Cajastac along Corralitos Creek, and the Calendaruc or Tiuvta at the mouth of the Pajaro River. Near Mission Santa Cruz between 1793 and 1795, the Charquin led a revolt with neighboring Sakian and Cuchillones ("Little Knives"), building traps and digging covered pits to capture the Spanish soldiers.

These 1940 photographs were taken on Emmet and School Streets in Santa Cruz, documenting the old cemetery grounds and neophyte housing from 1824, part of an adobe residence with 17 apartment quarters called the Neary-Rodiguez Building. After the building was remodeled in 1983 by Mission Santa Cruz California State Historic Park, it was completely recreated with original adobe bricks and finished with plaster.

This Victorian granite memorial of 1891, erected in front of the first adobe church site, honors those who settled the area. A longtime resident and donor of funds for a replica mission church built today's mission adjacent to the original property and the memorial. Gladys Sullivan, the benefactor, was niece of the late Sen. James D. Phelon. At the turn of the century she married Richard E. Doyle, an investment banker and a descendant of 1849 pioneer San Franciscans.

The 1876 Mission Santa Cruz painting above was researched by French artist Leon Trousset from surviving locals after gathering oral histories. He lived in Monterey and worked throughout the Southwest and Northern Mexico from the late 1860s to the early 1900s. Below is a modern postcard representing an artist's conception of Mission Santa Cruz as it appeared after 1795. A modern scale replica completed in 1931 stands today adjacent to the original mission site. (Below, author's collection.)

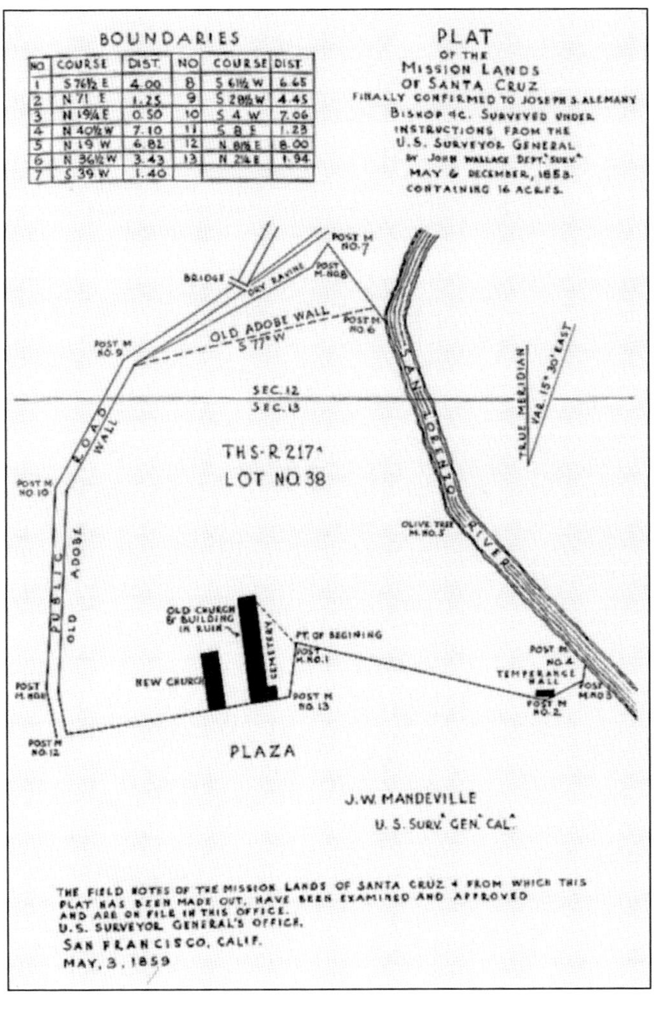

In 1857, the cornerstone was laid for a wooden church to replace the mission church. It served the parish until 1898, when it was torn down. In 1862, the Daughters of Charity of St. Vincent de Paul opened Holy Cross School, a day school and boarding school that was the first educational institution in the parish. In 1889, the present brick Gothic church was built. On September 25, 1891, the citizens of Santa Cruz erected a granite archway in front of the church to commemorate the founding of Mission Santa Cruz. New buildings graced the parish from the 1920s through the 1960s, including the high school and rectory. From 1982 to 1984, the interior of the church was renovated in preparation for the 1989 centennial. In 1989, the church was formally consecrated. Then on October 17, 1989, the earth shook again. The church was declared unsafe, and services were moved to the parish hall. On June 30, 1990, the parish hall itself burned down. Services were moved to the school courtyard and then into a tent pavilion.

Four

Frontier Refuge
Mission del Gloriosísima Patriarca San José

Fr. Fermín Francisco de Lasuén founded the 14th mission in Alta California, Mission del Gloriosísima Patriarca San José, on June 11, 1797, increasing Spain's settlements to secure the northern territories and eastern boundaries. No order came from the Spanish Crown for nearly six years after the founding of Nuestra Señora de la Soledad; then, in 1797, Mission San Jose became the first of five new missions constructed in one year. Only 12 miles east of Mission Santa Clara, the settlement was founded to honor Saint Joseph and to organize Indian neophytes from the Contra Costa region. A massive earthquake in October 1868 struck the mission, leaving only a part of the original adobe monastery wing salvageable. New restorations were completed in the 1930s. (Author's collection.)

Costeños or Coastoans come from many distinct tribes grouped together by the Spanish; 50 small communities with 40 to 400 denizens inhabited the coastal regions of Northern California from the San Francisco Bay to the Monterey Peninsula and Salinas Valley. Ludwig Andrevitch Choris depicted this group of six mission neophytes preparing for a ceremonial dance at Mission San Jose in 1806. Later, the church moved its Yokut and Ohlone neophytes to Mission Santa Clara de Asís. Then, following the natural pathways to the San Joaquin and Sacramento Valleys, missionaries succeeded in converting over 1,800 Yokut and Miwok east-bay neophytes by 1831.

This early photograph of Mission del Gloriosísima Patriarca San José was taken several years before the devastating earthquake of 1868. The early *campanario* at the left, and the large mission church, since destroyed, were attached to the convento to the right and still standing today, made from the original adobe bricks.

To the right side of Mission del Gloriosísima Patriarca San José, the adjoining monastery, pictured here during the late 1800s, is an original adobe building. Still standing today, the convento is used as a museum and as the entry to the mission grounds.

Mission del Gloriosísima Patriarca San José was located on the trails used to reach the remote interior and began housing Miwok and Yokut neophytes from the east bay in today's Fremont by 1815. This Thomas Houseworth stereo slide portrays the early adobe church buildings around 1866. Mission Santa Clara de Asís, 12 miles away, had continued attending to a large coastal native population.

The Mission del Gloriosísima Patriarca San José monastery wing, the entry to the mission grounds today, is pictured in 1906. The mission was located near the pass to the Coastal Range, now called Mission Pass, at a place named by the Oroysom natives. Arriving in June 1797, the scouts gathered materials for constructing a cross and an altar, and a crude thatched bower of branches was used as a shelter. (Southwest Museum of the American Indian Collection.)

Mission del Gloriosísima Patriarca San José lies 12 miles east of California's first city, El Pueblo de San José de Guadalupe, founded November 29, 1777, and served by Mission Santa Clara de Asís nearby. By the 1930s, the sign above the mission's convento mistakenly referred to the river near San Jose, the Guadalupe River, as the mission name. The error was corrected after modern restoration. (Above, author's collection; below, Santa Clara University Archives and Special Collections.)

Mission del Gloriosísima Patriarca San José's monastery wing is pictured around 1870.

A private chapel that served the convent of Dominican Sisters at Mission San Jose is pictured around 1935. An orphanage was erected in 1884 by Archbishop Joseph Sadoc Alemany as a seminary for young men studying for the priesthood and was offered to the Dominican Sisters as a boarding school.

Above is Mission San Jose's exterior before recent restorations replicated the original church of the 1830s at this site. Below, the entrance sign misnamed the mission, an error often copied in popular literature, replacing the mission's actual name, Mission del Gloriosísima Patriarca San José. (Below, Anderson family collection.)

Above, El Camino Real, "The Royal Way," led from Mission Santa Clara de Asís to Contra Costa, the opposite shore from San Francisco, and the Mission del Gloriosísima Patriarca San José on the eastern path to the San Joaquin River valley. The sign overhead in this 1930s photograph misnames the mission after Rio de Guadalupe. Below, a pioneer's tombstone at Mission San Jose's cemetery is seen. (Above, author's collection.)

Mission San Jose's monastery wing, constructed of adobe bricks, has survived earthquakes while the original construction at the adjoining mission church was destroyed. The church is located to the left and was entirely rebuilt between 1982 and 1985 as a replica of the original. Below is the mission convento or monastery wing as it appeared in the 1930s. (Below, Santa Clara University Archives and Special Collections.)

Streetcars in what is today the city of Fremont once ran past the Mission del Gloriosísima Patriarca San José in the 1930s. The mission was located about 12 miles from Mission Santa Clara de Asís on the trails going east to serve native environs. The friars recorded 1,886 neophytes living at the mission and 6,700 baptisms over the generations by 1831.

Simple posts lie on top of adobe walls, with redwood poles lashed by rawhide to support roof structures without nails. Similar construction techniques were used at Mission Dolores. (Southwest Museum of the American Indian Collection.)

The mission convento building has many adobe bricks from the original mission walls and an arcade consisting of simple wooden posts along the monastery wing at Mission del Gloriosísima Patriarca San José. Beginning in 1982 and completed in 1985, the Mission San Jose adobe church adjoining the convento was rebuilt to replicate its appearance of the 1830s.

This grave marker is dedicated to the Ohlone and thousands of neophytes who labored to build the Mission del Gloriosísima Patriarca San José of 1797 and 1805, the first structures of the padres' frontier settlement.

Five

Restoring the Sick
Mission San Rafael, Arcángel

Founded on December 14, 1817, Mission San Rafael, Arcángel, was first an asistencia for Mission Dolores and was built as a sanitarium. It was raised to full mission status in 1822. It was established as a health resort for ailing neophytes stricken by inhospitable cold living conditions or by the abuse encountered from Spanish soldiers at Yerba Buena. The mission was affected by the secularization laws of the Mexican Republic and then by neglect, as the buildings suffered invasive weathering, leaving "the mudheap," as it was known to locals, in ruins. The present day parish church of San Raphael was built in 1919, near the original mission site. (Author's collection.)

The mission church's star window was carried over to the main church influenced by Mission San Carlos Borromeo del Rio Carmelo, Father Serra's mission headquarters. Little was known about the original mission building itself except for descriptions of the interior and a few illustrations.

US Army captain John C. Fremont used the mission as a stable and shelter for his ragtag command of Americans with legendary scout Kit Carson around 1846, the year Commodore John Drake Sloat of the US Navy claimed California after the Battle of Monterey. Frémont would become a contender of Abraham Lincoln within the new Republican Party during its first presidential candidacy in 1856. (Author's collection.)

Fr. Luis Gil y Taboaoda, a Mexican Franciscan, was a skilled linguist who worked with the Coast Miwok, Pomo, and Wappo mission neophytes to construct the first adobes. The first chapel, a long and low building, had housed a room for sick neophytes with a dormitory. In this photograph, the parish church of St. Raphael from 1919, the turn-of-the-century signpost and bell marker, and the stone masonry walls are all elements enhancing the mission's place in California's unique history. (Author's collection.)

The neophytes at Mission San Rafael, Arcángel, were taught the skills of vaqueros—caring and herding cattle, horses, and sheep—as well as the farming of wheat, corn, beans, barley, and chickpeas. Living at the mission over 13 of its 17 years, Fr. Juan Amorós swore allegiance to Mexico. He reported over 1,000 neophytes living at the mission village. Two local chiefs became constant sources of trouble near the small mission and were captured and converted. One was a seafarer given the name Marin. The other, a renegade prisoner, Quintin, was captured by 1824. Both names survive in modern times as San Quentin and Marin County.

A sub-mission established as an asistencia of Mission Dolores, Mission San Rafael, Arcángel, was founded jointly by four Franciscan padres on December 14, 1817. Fathers Narcisco Durán of Mission San Jose, Ramón Abella of Mission Dolores, Luis Gil y Taboaoda, and Vincente Sarría took part in the founding ceremony. Within two years, Fr. Juan Amorós, a skilled carpenter, boat builder, and farmer, began a second, shorter and higher building, a mission church completed to the side of the original dormitory and dedicated in 1824. In later years, Don Mariano Guadalupe Vallejo, a retired general and autocratic leader in Northern California, acquired the mission rancho's neighboring Nacasio, and transplanted its grapevines, fruit trees, and livestock to his own extensive ranchos.

Saint Raphael, Archangel, was called "Healer of God." His name was given to the 1817 asistencia, founded as a hospital for ailing neophytes living just miles away at Mission San Francisco de Asís. The mixture of the Church of St. Raphael's Art Nouveau design and classic columns and arches support the massive campanile towering above. The church entry is guarded by the relief statue of Saint Rafael. The saint is one of seven archangels venerated in the scriptures, along with Saints Gabriel and Michael. The large church was remodeled and restored in 1926, 1949, and 1993. (Author's collection.)

The mission replica is seen on the right in this postcard view after its completion with funding by the Hearst Corporation in 1949. The parish church of St. Raphael's was constructed in 1919 adjacent to the original adobe mission. (Author's collection.)

This popular postcard depicts the old adobe Mission San Rafael, Arcángel, after 1824 with an L-shaped footprint. The artist, San Anselmo resident Felix Adrian Raynaud, had influenced the 1949 reconstruction using historical elements. The church was situated facing east towards the bay and sunrise. The orchards below are today the tall buildings of downtown San Rafael. (Author's collection.)

This postcard depicts the Mission San Rafael, Arcángel and the three original bells displayed on the wooden scaffold. The mission was under the care of Fr. Juan Amorós after Fr. Gil y Taboaoda, a Mexican friar, left in 1819. Father Amorós befriended the local natives and built the population of mission Indians to 1,140 by 1828. By 1829, a long-brewing feud between Mexican soldiers and the natives came to battle, and neophytes protected the beloved Father Amorós during heated exchanges lasting for weeks, hiding him in distant marshlands. He later recovered the mission and restored it, living there until his death in 1832. He is buried in the mission chapel. (Author's collection.)

Six

THE PASSING ERA
MISSION SAN FRANCISCO SOLANO

Fr. José Altimira, a young, ambitious Franciscan, believed in preserving the sacred traditions of the Franciscan Alta California missions. He proposed closing Mission Dolores and Mission San Rafael, Arcángel, replacing them with the new Mission San Francisco Solano in 1823. The Sonoma mission was named for Saint Francis Solano (1549–1610), a Spanish friar and Peruvian missionary, and consecrated in Sonoma, the "Valley of the Moon," to help avoid the frequent sickness borne by native neophyte populations. Approval had come from the first Mexican-born Californian governor, Luis Antonio Argüello, using legislative procedures to create the new mission in the northernmost frontier. With a compromise at the close of the Mexican War of Independence in 1821, mission president Fr. José Señán ordered Mission San Francisco de Asís and Mission San Rafael, Arcángel, to continue and Father Altimira's mission to be added as the last in a 54-year lineage. (Author's collection.)

This postcard from 1934 depicts the coastal settlement at Fort Ross on the Sonoma Coast. The outpost was historically a Russian stockade established on September 10, 1812. The settlement became the northern boundary of Spanish territorial claims in Alta California just 65 miles from San Francisco. The seaside shelter provided a home for 260 settlers at its peak, and a few natives were baptized into the Eastern Orthodox faith while living among the Russian settlers. Spanish Franciscan father Mariano Payéras entered into his diary, "the northern corner of the square mounts five cannons on two floors, and another bastion in the southern corner mounting four cannons." Also commenting was Mariano G. Vallejo, who reported in 1833, "In the two corners opposite each other, one overlooking the mountains and the other overlooking the sea, are mounted 12 pieces of artillery up in two towers or lookout platforms. Each piece is of eight caliber and six are located in each tower." In late 1841, Capt. John Sutter agreed to buy the Russian-American Company's assets from Alexander Rotchev at Fort Ross, and on January 1, 1842, about 100 colonists departed from Bodega Bay, returning to their distant homeland. The final sale of the Fort Ross colony included all buildings, livestock, and implements as claimed by the Mexican Republic. (Author's collection.)

A full family portrait made before 1880 displays General Vallejo at an advanced age in a more modern era. In 1834, Gov. José Figueroa ordered Lt. Mariano Guadalupe Vallejo, commandant of the San Francisco Presidio, to begin secularizing the missions. He was granted 44,000 acres from the California governor; 22,000 acres were added later to compensate him for his services. (Sonoma County Historical Society/Depot Park Museum.)

Fr. José Altimira, in the tradition of the Franciscan missionaries, came to northern Alta California and raised a large cross, conducting the first mass at the station in Sonoma he called "New San Francisco" on July 4, 1823.

A jubilant celebration commemorating the Bear Flag Revolt's 50th anniversary was recorded with a panoramic camera on June 13, 1896, in Sonoma Square. The historical gathering celebrated

This photograph of a new 1928 Hudson and its owner was taken from one of two recently rediscovered glass plates. The car is parked in front of the last link of California's mission heritage sites. (Anderson family collection.)

three survivors and nearly five decades of American statehood. (Robert Parmelee Collection, Sonoma County Historical Society/Depot Park Museum.)

After 61 years, the raising of the Bear Flag was commemorated by Henry Beeson, the lone survivor from the original 33 men summoned by American captain John C. Frémont. The Bear Flag Revolt of 1846 captured General Vallejo at his headquarters and removed him from power. Mission San Francisco Solano had been dedicated on July 4, 1823, and continued to colonize the natives. A third mission church had been built by General Vallejo in 1840 and is fully restored today. (Sonoma County Historical Society/Depot Park Museum.)

The 50th anniversary of the Bear Flag Revolt was celebrated at the Sonoma Plaza on June 13, 1896. A mast was raised (center) for a commemorative flag. In 1903, the California Historical Landmarks League rescued several buildings at Mission San Francisco Solano, purchased later by William

Declared unsafe and a nuisance in 1940, the old adobe had a diverse history as General Vallejo's personal jail at his property just three blocks north of the Sonoma Plaza. The building was also used as a gatehouse for his residence. (Robert Parmelee Collection, Sonoma County Historical Society/Depot Park Museum.)

Randolph Hearst. The old adobe chapel (to the right, not pictured) was covered with brick veneer in 1860, and the steeple was added in 1857. The convento wing was used for wine storage in 1880. (Robert Parmelee Collection, Sonoma County Historical Society/Depot Park Museum.)

Located northeast of the Sonoma Plaza, the mission forms part of the Sonoma Historic Park complex of buildings and sites. East Spain Street runs east and west along the front of the property; First Street East runs along the western edge. (Southwest Museum of the American Indian Collection.)

In a painting by Oriana Day of the 1830s version of the Sonoma Plaza with El Casa Grande, the immense military structure is accurately portrayed adjacent to the Sonoma mission with several wooden structures including a granary, a house for the priests, and seven houses for the guards and their families. The first adobe buildings to house the padres were completed by 1824. (Southwest Museum of the American Indian Collection.)

Three surviving members of the Bear Flag Revolt of 1846 would meet again during the 50th anniversary. From left to right are Henry Beeson of Booneville, Benjamin Dewell of Upper Lake, and Harvey Porterfield of Napa. This commemorative photograph was taken within the garden of Porterfield's home. (Sonoma County Historical Society/Depot Park Museum.)

A March 1946 celebration brought Leo Carrillo (right), the famous western actor, State Parks commissioner, and descendant of Spanish Californians, to raise the old Bear Flag during jubilant celebrations with Gov. Earl Warren (left) and Sen. Herbert Slater. This was a fundraiser for the historic 100th anniversary of the American revolt's commemoration, held a month later. (Robert Parmelee Collection, Sonoma County Historical Society/Depot Park Museum.)

This whimsical portrait in bucolic Sonoma was taken at the rear of the mission courtyard well before many private houses and streets were developed.

The turn-of-the-century Mission Play celebrants pose in elaborate 19th-century garb. The play was performed at different venues throughout California. The story commemorated the missions' full history and the later rise of the Mexican Republic in 1831. (Sonoma County Historical Society/ Depot Park Museum.)

A 1912 collapse led to the restoration of the Vallejo Chapel, removing its brick veneer and inaccurate 1857 steeple profile. The renovations continued until the smooth adobe finish with plaster application accurately resembled the original mission of the 1840s.

Fr. José Gutierrez was stationed at the Sonoma mission for a short time and was succeeded by Fr. José Lorenzo de la Concepcion Quijas in 1834. Father Quijas later transferred to Mission San Jose in 1843. The property was purchased by the Historical Landmark League in 1903 and a full restoration was completed in 1913.

Mission San Francisco Solano de Sonoma claimed many thousands of acres of agricultural land operated by many neophyte and Spanish families. They farmed cattle and horses as far north as Santa Rosa. The mission chapel had stood a little over 25 years before the Treaty of Guadalupe Hidalgo in 1848, which ended the Mexican American War.

After 1834, all missions had been closed by the Mexican government, leaving the church without a regular spiritual leader. Father Quijas, and later, a lineage of priests, made occasional forays to Sonoma to celebrate mass in the old adobe church.

In 1862, question of mission land ownership was officially settled, and the archbishop was granted the church property and padres' house area (the current mission grounds) amounting to 2.06 acres, plus a vineyard to the east. The Catholic Church continued to hold the property until 1881, after which the land was sold to a local merchant and replaced by a new parish church building half a mile west.

The mission was designated California Historical Monument No. 3 in 1926. Restoration work had begun, and by 1943–1944, tile-topped perimeter walls were constructed to enclose today's somewhat smaller courtyard. An adjacent 0.91-acre parcel north of the mission site was later purchased and added to the park. (Above, Southwest Museum of the American Indian Collection.)

The Vallejo Chapel became a full parish church of Mission San Francisco Solano in Sonoma in 1834. Modernization undertaken in 1858 included a brick facade covering the entire chapel exterior, modern shingles, and a new wooden belfry. Its outer facade offered added protection to the adobe brick walls, but in time, few original walls remained standing except parts of the convento wing walls.

Photographed at the mission's front, a symbol of 54 years of history as a Spanish settlement, the actors of the Mission Play marked Sonoma's historical significance. A celebration of the passing era was reenacted with the Mission Play, created in 1911 by Stephen McGroarty. The popular play depicted Father Serra's establishment of the Alta California mission chain, reminiscing on its last days and final mission. (Sonoma County Historical Society/Depot Park Museum.)

By the time of this 1960s postcard, Mission San Francisco Solano de Sonoma was surrounded by Sonoma County wineries and had become a popular historical attraction to visitors making stops in the rural countryside.

This vintage photograph of Mission San Francisco Solano de Sonoma's Vallejo Chapel of 1840 depicts a modernized adobe church with brick facing, with the early convento wing remaining from the 1880s.

In 1834, the Mexican government began enforcing secularization, ultimately affecting all missions. Capt. John C. Frémont arrived at Mission San Rafael, Arcángel, ready to stand against the Mexican military of General Vallejo. With no opposition, he continued a march south and camped with his battalion in January 1847, meeting California's Mexican governor Pio Pico. Upon the signing of the Treaty of Campo de Cahuenga, all serious hostilities ended against Mexico with the United States' conquest of California.

In 1834, General Vallejo had been ordered to map El Pueblo de Sonoma as eight-acre tracts including Mission San Francisco Solano. The town has had many historical buildings, and several remain today. By 1839, the mission complex, including a large adobe church, began to decay. The building materials were in great demand and were distributed throughout the community.

In 1835, Vallejo laid out the new streets using the mission as a starting point. His own pre-fabricated home was shipped around Cape Horn and brought to Sonoma, then built within walking distance of the Sonoma Plaza.

General Vallejo's pivotal role in the history of California occurred through the state's transition from a Spanish possession to the Mexican Republic in 1821 and finally to the United States in 1850. (Sonoma County Historical Society/Depot Park Museum.)

Gen. Mariano Guadalupe Vallejo's ranch home is the largest domestic adobe remaining in the United States and is located in Petaluma. In the style of a Monterey Colonial, it served as the center of General Vallejo's 66,000-acre (100 square miles) working ranch between 1836 and 1846. He employed 2,000 Indians to complete one large L-shaped building rather than constructing a number of smaller working areas.

In 1910, the remainder of General Vallejo's vast adobe ranch house was purchased by the Native Sons of the Golden West, Petaluma Parlor No. 27. In 1932, it was registered as a California State Historical Landmark, and the adobe home was registered as a National Historic Landmark in 1970.

Gen. Mariano Vallejo was born in Monterey in 1807 and was appointed as administrator of the mission lands by 1831; then, he was ordered to enforce the secular laws enacted by the Mexican congress.

Over time, half of the grand Petaluma adobe ranch building has succumbed to neglect and the forces of nature. It was preserved as a centerpiece of Petaluma Adobe State Historic Park and museum. About 80 percent of its adobe bricks are original, although most of the wood has been replaced. The eastern foundations are no longer standing and have deteriorated into half-visible walls.

This view from the rear of Mission San Francisco Solano's convento and chapel was photographed around 1934, before modern restorations were completed to the courtyard. After the Bear Flag Revolt, General Vallejo was imprisoned at Sutter's Fort in Sacramento for two months. On July 7, 1846, Commodore John Drake Sloat landed his men in the harbor of Monterey, raising the American flag and taking formal possession.

Initially, local Indians were hostile to the new mission, attacking the settlement in 1826. Shortly afterwards, its discouraged founder, Father Altimira, asked to be transferred south. Padre Buenaventura Fortuni was assigned to take his place. In a painting California artist Oriana Weatherbee Day made between 1877 and 1884, the earliest mission church at Mission San Francisco Solano de Sonoma is portrayed during a neophyte Indian ceremony.

Seven

MISSIONS PAST AND PRESENT
TOURING EL CAMINO REAL

Mission San Francisco de Asís, sixth in the line of original Spanish missions, was founded on June 29, 1776, by Fr. Francisco Palóu, the longtime companion and biographer of Fr. Junípero Serra, the patron of the Spanish missions of Alta California. Father Serra, gazing upon the shores of the great bay, gave praise: "Thanks be to God that now our father St. Francis with the Holy Cross of the Procession of Missions has reached the last limit of the Californian continent." The sixth California mission was founded by Father Junípero Serra in 1776. The mission is located at 3321 Sixteenth Street, San Francisco, CA 94114, and can be contacted at 415-621-8203 or www.missiondolores.org. (Author's collection.)

In 1995, a concrete duplicate of the baptismal font from the Church of St. Peter's in Petra, Majorca, where Fr. Junípero Serra was baptized, was placed in a niche at Mission San Francisco de Asís. Mission Dolores was visited by Father Serra after two exploratory ventures to San Francisco's hills with Lt. José Joaquín Moraga to begin preparing the site for the present church. (Author's collection.)

Gaspar de Portolá named a small stream running to a lake and then to the bay Arroyo de Nuestra Señora de los Dolores, honoring Our Lady of Sorrows; Seven Sorrows are depicted on each of two side balconies, with another in a carving over the main door at the rear of the church. The walls and side altars have fine examples of Mexican statuary, like this statue of Saint Francis, and date as early as 1810. (Author's collection.)

The hand-carved altar and reredos decorated with gold leaf is possibly the finest example of Spanish baroque decorative art of all the missions. It was brought from Mexico in 1796. Fr. Francisco Palóu was the founding friar, celebrating the first mass under a makeshift shelter in 1776, just five days before the signing of the Declaration of Independence in Philadelphia. (Author's collection.)

Within the walls of the Mission Dolores cemetery are memorials to the many pioneers, friars, and Indians who were part of the mission's history throughout the centuries. The local Olhone working at the mission erected a tule hut and a memorial to the past and to their thousands of elders buried at the mission; it is on display in the cemetery. (Author's collection.)

Mission Santa Clara is the eighth of California's 21 missions, founded in 1777. It is the centerpiece of Santa Clara University and historically the first mission of the south San Francisco Bay area. The mission is located at 500 E. El Camino Real, Santa Clara, CA 95053. It can be contacted at 408-554-4356 or www.scu.edu/visitors/mission. (Author's collection.)

This original adobe wall is a remainder of the deteriorated quadrangle walls from 1825, still standing after fires and earthquakes. The first and second mission buildings were located on the banks of the Guadalupe River but were swept away after severe flooding, after which the mission moved to its present site. The Adobe Lodge connected to the wall is a restaurant open to the public. (Author's collection.)

The garden to the rear of the mission church displays mature grapevines, olives, several palm varieties, and many native plants. The serene campus of Santa Clara University has an arboretum-like setting. (Author's collection.)

In 1926, at 7:00 am, a fire broke out in the bell tower of the remodeled church. To the screams of sirens, priests and students fought in their nightshirts to save the church and relics within, but the building was fully destroyed. Only one of the original bells from 1799 was recovered intact; a replacement was sent by King Alfonso XIII of Spain in 1929, the year of the new church's completion. (Author's collection.)

Today's church nave at Mission Santa Clara de Asís is bright and decorative, in tribute to the neophytes under the direction of Augustin Dávila, an artist from Mexico. After the fire of 1926, the reredos and its statues were restored to match the originals, and the ceiling above the sanctuary was repainted to simulate the Dávila design. (Author's collection.)

The reredos was rebuilt to match the original destroyed in the fire of 1926. At a side altar, the crucifix saved from the fire is displayed as it was in the original church. The modern architecture of the church, embellished by Victorian elements, largely reflects the early church interior as it was built in 1825. (Author's collection.)

Mission La Exaltacion de la Santa Cruz was founded by Fr. Fermín Francisco de Lasuén on August 28, 1791, in honor of the Holy Cross. The 12th mission of Alta California, it was destroyed by the earthquake of 1857 and rebuilt at one third its original size as a replica mission, completed in 1931 at Emmet and School Streets, 200 feet from the original site. It is located in Santa Cruz Mission State Historic Park, 144 School St., Santa Cruz, CA 95060. It can be contacted at 831-425-5849 or www.parks.ca.gov. (Author's collection.)

On October 17, 1989, the earth shook and the church was declared unsafe, and services were moved to the parish hall. On June 30, 1990, a fire devastated the parish hall. Today it has been retrofitted and rebuilt, along with the convent and the mission chapel. A historic garden was begun over the old mission burial grounds. (Author's collection.)

Mission Santa Cruz today resembles the decaying church drawn prior to the earthquake of 1857 by artist Henry Miller, who observed, "a number of ancient adobe houses, occupied principally by natives, however are unoccupied at present." A former two-story building, converted to the Eagle Hotel, was the largest building within the Santa Cruz Mission quadrangle and once housed the Santa Cruz courthouse. (Author's collection.)

The Neary-Rodriguez Adobe has been continuously occupied from the Spanish era to the present. It served as Native American neophyte family housing, with one family assigned to each of the original 17 rooms. This is the only example of its kind still standing in California today. (Author's collection.)

The 14th Spanish mission of Alta California, located today in the East Bay area, was founded by Fr. Fermín Francisco de Lasuen in 1797. Old Mission San Jose is located at 43300 Mission Blvd., Fremont, CA 94539. It can be contacted at 510-657-1797 or www.missionsanjose.org. (Author's collection.)

Several hundred Ohlone natives came to live at Mission San Jose after the founding and began a new way of life, as thousands of cattle roamed the mission ranges. Acres of wheat and other crops were planted and harvested under the direction of the padres. (Author's collection.)

The Ohlone, the predominant coastal native tribe of the Bay Area, lived in harmony with the ancient forests, ocean, and nature, and their food included seeds, roots, berries, acorn meal, small game, and seafood. (Author's collection.)

The trail of early travelers to the Livermore Valley and the San Joaquin Valley led past Mission San Jose, and the friars ventured farther and farther east, gathering new converts. Today's church is open to the public and offers concerts throughout the year. (Author's collection.)

The 20th Alta California mission was founded by Fr. Vicente de Sarría in 1817, named for the Archangel Raphael. On October 19, 1822, San Rafael was declared independent of Mission Dolores and raised to full mission stature. A replica of Mission San Rafael, Arcángel, was completed in 1949, generously supported by the Hearst Foundation. The mission is located at 1104 Fifth Avenue, San Rafael, CA 94901 and can be contacted at 415-454-8141 or www.saintraphael.com. (Author's collection.)

Pio Pico, the last Mexican governor of California, sold Mission San Rafael, Arcángel, in 1843, then cancelled the sale, allowing plundering by settlers including Mariano Vallejo, the head *comandante*. The mission lands extended as far north as Bodega Bay, with Spanish presence meant to prevent Russian settlers moving south from Fort Ross. (Author's collection.)

The mission has neither a bell tower nor bell wall; traditionally, the scaffolding was near the door of the mission church. From the earliest sketch by General Vallejo, there was a bell suspended from an L-shaped post at the original church. (Author's collection.)

Mission San Rafael, Arcángel, was founded on December 14, 1817, by Fr. Vicente de Sarria under the patronage of San Rafael, Arcángel. It provided a location for neophytes to recuperate from the damp, harsh climate of Mission San Francisco de Asís. Within a year, the asistencia had a population of over 300; eventually, more than 1,000 lived at the grounds. (Author's collection.)

St. Raphael Church became a parish in 1884, and the new church was completed in 1919. The large church has been remodeled and restored as recently as 1993. (Author's collection.)

Mission San Francisco Solano was the final Spanish mission of Alta California. The 21st California mission was founded in 1823 by Fr. José Altimira and named for St. Francis Solano, a missionary to the Peruvian Indians. The mission was purchased by the William R. Hearst Landmarks League in 1903 and completely restored after 1913. It became a California state historic park in 1927 and is located at 20 E. Spain Street, Sonoma, CA 95476. It can be contacted at 707-938-1519 or www.parks.ca.gov. (Author's collection.)

The peal of the 1811 bell of Mission San Francisco Solano was heard over the 10,000 acres of the mission property. Mission San Francisco Solano's station originally was planned as a replacement for Mission San Francisco de Asís after a steady decline of the neophyte native population, which succumbed to the harsh climate and European illnesses over decades. (Author's collection.)

The altar of the Vallejo Chapel at Mission San Francisco Solano was built by 1841 to serve the young pueblo of Sonoma. Today the monastery wing is a museum, and the adjacent adobe, the old soldiers' barracks, is run by California State Historic Parks. (Author's collection.)

Located at East Spain and First Streets on the northeast corner of the Sonoma Plaza, the mission has gone through many renovations before being fully restored to its 1841 design, as it was during Vallejo's era. The bell marker was placed in 1909. (Author's collection.)

The original mission chapel of redwood was built on the opposite side of the convento wing at the eastern corner and served during the first years. It was dedicated April 4, 1824, with 26 Miwok children baptized; over 900 joined the church during its 11-year history. (Author's collection.)

The courtyard's prickly pear cactus is the site of the original *monjerio*, or quarters for the neophyte women. Beyond the courtyard were enterprises including a tannery, hide vats, vineyards, orchards, crops, and livestock. (Author's collection.)

The Vallejo Chapel at Mission San Francisco Solano was built in 1840 and rebuilt matching the original in natural decorative tones used by natives from vegetable and root sources. Visit the mission at Sonoma State Historic Park at 363 Third Street West in Sonoma or call 707-938-9560. (Author's collection.)

Pathfinders of early California trails marched the 650 miles of El Camino Real, the "King's Highway," connecting the 21 legendary Spanish missions. Franciscan friars had planned the mission system, and the Spanish viceroy imported craftsmen and settlers from Mexico up the supply route from San Blas and Baja, essential in keeping the new colonies productive.

BIBLIOGRAPHY

Berger, John A. *The Franciscan Missions of California.* Garden City, NY: Doubleday & Co., 1948.

Chapman, Charles E. *A History of California: The Spanish Period.* New York: The Macmillan Co., 1921.

Elder, Paul. *The Old Spanish Missions of California.* San Francisco: Paul Elder and Co., 1913.

Forbes, Jack G. *Native Americans of California and Nevada.* Happy Camp, CA: Naturegraph Publishers, 1982.

Gudde, Erwin G. *1000 Place Names.* Berkeley and Los Angeles: University of California Press, 1965.

Hoover, Mildred Brooke, Hero Eugene Rensch, and Ethel Grace. *Historic Spots in California.* Stanford, CA: Stanford University Press, 1953.

Kimbro, Edna E. and Julia G. Costello with Tevvy Ball. *The Missions of California.* Los Angeles: J. Paul Getty Museum, 2009.

Morgado, Martin J. *Junípero Serra: A Pictorial Biography.* Monterey, CA: Siempre Adelante Publishing, 1991.

Mornin, Edward and Lorna Mornin. *Saints of California.* Los Angeles: J. Paul Getty Museum, 2009.

Sunset Editors. *The California Missions: A Pictorial History.* Menlo Park, CA: Sunset Publishing Corp., 1991.

Wright, Ralph B. *California's Missions.* Los Angeles: Sterling Press, 1950.

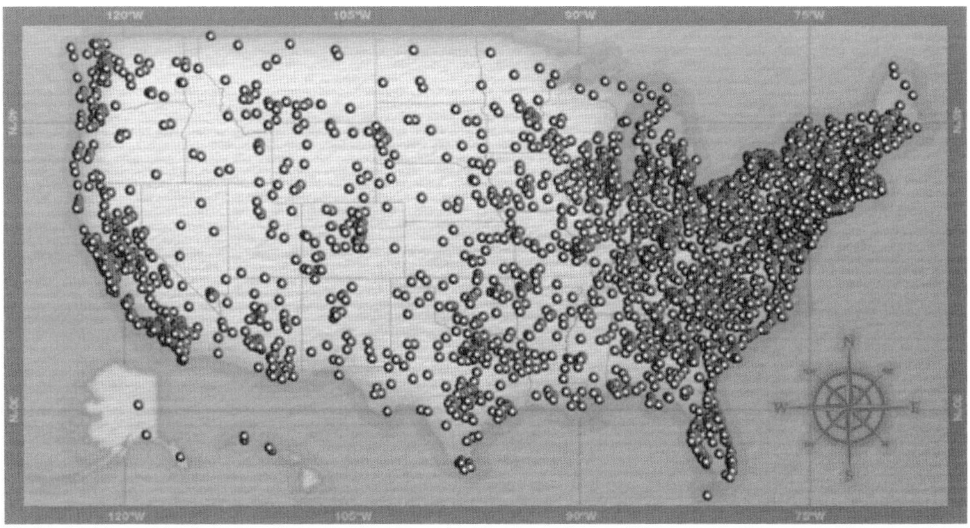